RATHER
Obscure
VICTORIAN
Limericks

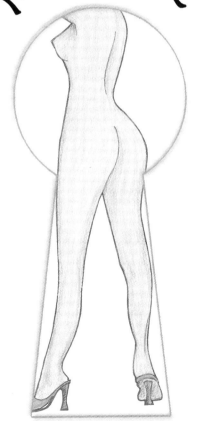

Brian A. Lee - Blackmore

blished in the UK by
)WERFRESH Limited
nit 3, Everdon Park,
eartlands Industrial Estate,
aventry
N11 5YJ

lephone   01327 871 777
csimile   01327 879 222
Mail info@powerfresh.co.uk

BN   1904967264

rinted in Slovakia By Polygraf / Production service ZoneS
owerfresh   July 2005

The truest observation about limericks was actually made in a limerick:

A limerick packs laughs anatomical
Into space that is quite economical.
But the good ones I've seen
So seldom are clean,
And the clean ones so seldom are comical.

Why perfect alliteration and hysterically funny punch lines are common factors in what are viewed by many as highly obscene and disgusting rhymes is often to do with the fact that the obscene Limerick is in reality the most widespread. The proliferation of this form of five line nonsense verse was the greater because Limericks easily lend themselves to composition by those who would ordinarily have little poetic ability. From bakers to bricklayers — everyone can do it. Likewise, they are an ideal platform for those with some talent, education and a broad vocabulary. Curates and Cardinals are as much culprits in this as their lesser brethren. As such, out of the millions of Limericks that have been composed since the end of the 19th century (and the Victorian and Edwardian Limerick predominates here), the larger number of brilliant, well-formed and superbly rhythmical examples are obscene. That so many persist, as a form of social communication, is testament to the fact that there is much humour and enjoyment to be found in them. This remains true irrespective of, and perhaps despite the fact that, they are undeniably obscene and sometimes relate to things that we find abhorrent, distasteful or unsettling. The fact is, this aspect is often softened by the shear brilliance of the compositional approach. In the best ones the crudity and obscenity become incidental, and we stand amazed and entertained by the 'laughs anatomical' in a 'space economical'.

Though coarseness and vulgarity win easily in terms of the social retention and longevity of such verse, it is not essential, and there are a number of equally admirable Limericks which are able to incorporate all the qualities of the best without resorting to anything crude or offensive. Of these, this collection includes a few of those better known. Recognized as witty and clever, these particular examples demonstrate that there is not a complete dearth of comparable cleverness.

It would be quite naive to assume that these five line verses were originated wholly by Edward Lear in his Book of Nonsense in 1846 although the word Limerick might well be a corruption of "Learick". However, there appear to be earlier historical precedents, there being some evidence that the form was known as early as the 1690's. At that time, soldiers of the "Irish Brigade", who were recruited in the town of Limerick and sent to France, eventually brought back a type of five line verse already popular at the time and similar to a French verse form and the English nursery rhyme. Indeed, the English nursery rhyme, such as *Hickory, Dickory, Dock* - etc, is a close relative as a five line rhyme but antedates any limerick *per se* by hundreds of years. As the years passed, the five line verse took on a persuasive popularity whether obscene or not. Party games and national competitions in the late 19th and early part of the 20th centuries extemporizing on a pre-set pair of lines, have also been a rich and fertile source of limericks. Strange it is, that the most durable appear to be those which are risqué, and the best of those the ones which take us to the edge of tolerance and acceptance and yet redeem themselves as admirable pieces of humour or poetry.

As a note to the reader, these examples herein are as found or learnt by the author, either through word of mouth or in the numerous British and US anthologies and collections that have appeared in the past. Not only is this selection a perspective on the variety of forms to be found, it confirms that there are likely to be many versions of one particular Limerick in circulation. This can be confusing since, too often, lines of one may be borrowed from another or the pattern of rhyme or alliteration is similar.

Where possible in this collection, the original has been used though it remains true that later, or alternative, versions may be more polished and elegant. Finally, there are many, many examples that have been excluded because they rely too much on profanities, obscenities and blasphemy or reflect too much a disturbed mind. The criteria we set are simple, is it funny, is it clever, does it show merit above its vulgarity? If so, you will find it here!

Brian. A. Lee-Blackmore 2004

From deep in the crypt at St. Giles
Came a bellow that echoed for miles.
Said the rector, "My gracious,
Has Father Ignatius
Forgotten the Bishop has piles!?"

There once was a dentist named Stone
Who saw all his patients alone.
In a fit of depravity
He filled the wrong cavity,
And my, how his practice has grown!

There once was a man from Sydney
Who could put it up to her kidney.
But the man from Quebec
Put it up to her neck;
He had a big one, now didn't he?

There once was a man named McSweeny
Who spilled lots of gin on his weeney
So just to be couth
He added vermouth
And slipped his best girl a martini.

There once was a woman from Arden
Who sucked off a man in a garden.
He said, "My dear Flo,
Where does all that stuff go?"
And she said, "[Swallow hard] " beg pardon?"

There once was a young man named Gene,
Who invented a screwing machine.
Concave and convex,
It served either sex,
And it played with itself in-between.

There was a gay parson of Norton
Whose prick, although thick, was a short 'un.
To make up for this loss,
He had balls like a horse,
And never spent less than a quartern.

There was a young fellow named Blaine,
And he screwed some disgusting old Jane.
She was ugly and smelly
With an awful pot-belly,
But... well, they were caught in the rain.

There was a young fellow named Sweeney,
Whose girl was a terrible meanie,
The hatch of her snatch,
Had a catch that would latch,
She could only be screwed by Houdini.

There was a young girl from Decatur
Who was had by a large alligator.
But no one quite knew
How she relished that screw,
For after he screwed her, he ate her.

There was a young girl from Peru,
Who had nothing whatever to do.
So she sat on the stairs,
And counted cunt hairs,
Four thousand, three hundred and two.

There was a young girl of East Lynne
Whose mother, to save her from sin,
Had filled up her crack,
To the brim with shellac,
But the boys picked it out with a pin.

There was a young girl of Detroit
Who at fucking was very adroit:
She could squeeze her vagina
To a pin-point, or finer,
Or open it out like a quoit.

And she had a friend named Durand
Whose cock could contract or expand.
He could diddle a midge
Or the arch of a bridge —
Their performance together was grand!

There was a young girl of Mobile,
Who hymen was made of chilled steel,
To give her a thrill,
Take a rotary drill,
Or a number nine emery wheel.

There was a young girl of Penzance
Who boarded a bus in a trance.
The passengers fucked her,
Likewise the conductor,
While the driver shot off in his pants.

There was a young girl of Spitzbergen,
Whose people all thought her a virgin,
Till they found her in bed
With her twat very red,
And the head of a kid just emergin'.

There was a young lad name of Durcan
Who was always jerkin' his gherkin.
His father said, "Durcan!
Stop jerkin' your gherkin!
Your gherkin's for ferkin', not jerkin'.

There was a young lady at sea
Who said, "God, how it hurts me to pee."
"I see," said the mate,
"That accounts for the state
Of the captain, the purser, and me."

There was a young lady from Wheeling
Who had a peculiar feeling.
She laid on her back
And tickled her crack
And pissed all over the ceiling.

There was a young lady named Gloria
Who was had by Sir Gerald Du Maurier,
And then by six men,
Sir Gerald again,
And the band at the Waldorf-Astoria.

There was a young lady of Natchez
Who chanced to be born with two snatches,
And she often said, "Shit!
Why, I'd give either tit
For a man with equipment that matches."

There was a young lady of Wheeling
Who professed to lack sexual feeling.
But a cynic named Boris
Just touched her clitoris,
And she had to be scraped off the ceiling.

There was a young man from Bombay
Who fashioned a cunt out of clay
But the heat of his prick
Turned it into a brick
And rubbed all his foreskin away.

There was a young man from Boston
Who rode around in an Austin.
There was room for his ass
And a gallon of gas,
But his balls hung out and he lost 'em.

There was a young man of Kildare
Who was fucking a girl on the stair.
The banister broke,
But he doubled his stroke
And finished her off in mid-air.

There was a young man of Lahore
Whose prick was one inch and no more.
It was all right for key-holes
And young girl's pee-holes,
But not worth a damn with a whore.

There was a young man with a fiddle
Who asked of his girl, "Do you diddle?"
She replied, "Yes, I do,
But prefer to with two —
It's twice as much fun in the middle."

There was a young man with a prick
Which into his wife he would stick
Every morning and night
If it stood up all right —
Not a very remarkable trick.

His wife had a nice little cunt:
It was hairy, and soft, and in front,
And with this she would fuck him,
Though sometimes she'd suck him —
A charming, if commonplace, stunt.

There was a young man with one foot
Who had a very long root.
If he used this peg
As an extra leg
Is a question exceedingly moot.

There was a young miss from Johore
Who'd lie on a mat on the floor;
In a manner uncanny
She'd wobble her fanny,
And drain your nuts dry to the core.

There was a young monk from Siberia
Whose life got drearia' and drearia'
Till he did to a nun
What shouldn't be done
And made her a mother superia'.

There was a young monk from Tibet
And this is the damnedest one yet
His cock was so long
And incredibly strong
That he buggered six Greeks en brochette.

There was a young parson of Harwich,
Tried to grind his betrothed in a carriage.
She said, "No, you young goose,
Just try self-abuse.
And the other we'll try after marriage."

There was a young peasant named Gorse
Who fell madly in love with his horse.
Said his wife, "You rapscallion,
That horse is a stallion —
This constitutes grounds for divorce."

There was a young person of Kent
Who was famous wherever he went.
All the way through a fuck,
He would quack like a duck,
And he crowed like a cock when he spent.

There was a young physicist named Fisk
Whose lovemaking was rather brisk.
So quick was his action,
The Lorentz Contraction
Shortened his rod to a disc !!

There was a young plumber named Lee
Who was plumbing his girl by the sea.
She said, "Stop your plumbing,
There's somebody coming"
Said the plumber, still plumbing, "It's me."

There was a young royal marine,
Who tried to fart "God Save the Queen".
When he reached the soprano
Out came only guano
And his britches weren't fit to be seen.

There was a young sailor from Brighton,
Who remarked to his girl, "You're a tight one."
She replied, "'Pon my soul,
You're in the wrong hole;
There's plenty of room in the right one."

There was a young Sapphic named Anna
Who stuffed her friend's cunt with banana,
Which she sucked, bit by bit,
From her partner's warm slit,
In the most approved lesbian manner.

There was a young Scot in Madrid
Who got fifty-five fucks for a quid.
When they said, "Are you faint?"
He replied, "No, I ain't,
But I don't feel as good as I did."

There was a young student from Yale
Who was getting his first piece of tail.
He shoved in his pole,
But in the wrong hole,
And a voice from beneath yelled: "No sale!"

There was a young whore from Kaloo
Who filled her vagina with glue.
She said with a grin,
"If they pay to get in,
They can pay to get out again too!"

There was a young woman called Pearl
Who quite resembled a churl;
When she asked sex-mad Tex
Whether he would like to have sex,
"Certainly," he cried "Who's the girl?"

There was a young woman in Dee
Who stayed with each man she did see.
When it came to a test
She wished to be best,
And practice makes perfect, you see.

There was a young woman named Alice
Who peed in a Catholic chalice.
She said, "I do this
From a great need to piss,
And not from sectarian malice."

There was a young woman named Florence
Who for fucking professed an abhorrence,
But they found her in bed
With her cunt flaming red,
And her poodle-dog spending in torrents.

There was a young woman named Sutton
Who said, as she carved up the mutton,
"My father preferred
The last sheep in the herd —
This is one of his children I'm cuttin'."

There was a young girl from the Creek,
Who's periods came three times a week,
"How very provoking."
Said the doctor near choking,
"There's no time for poking, so to speak."

There was a young woman of Cheadle,
Who once gave the clap to a beadle.
Said she, "Does it itch?"
"It does, you damned bitch,
And it burns like hell-fire when I peedle."

There was a young woman of Condover
Whose husband had ceased to be fond of 'er.
Her pussy was juicy,
Her arse soft and goosey,
But peroxide had now made a blonde of 'er.

There was a young girl named Louise,
With a marvelous vaginal squeeze,
She inspired such pleasure,
In her lovers stiff measure
That she caused his untimely decease.

There was a young woman of Croft
Who played with herself in a loft,
Having reasoned that candles
Could never cause scandals,
Besides which they did not go soft.

Said another young woman of Croft,
Amusing herself in the loft,
"A salami or wurst
Is what I'd choose first —
With bologna you know you've been boffed."

Said His Worship "Now Mary O'Morgan,
Did the prisoner uncover his organ,
Said Mary "I'm not sure,
Never seen one before,
But t'was more like a flute than an organ."

There was a young maid of Asturious,
Whose temper was frantic and furious,
She used to thrown figs,
At gentlemen's dicks,
A habit unseemly, but curious.

There was a young woman, quite handsome,
Who got stuck in a sleeping room transom.
When she offered much gold
For release, she was told
That the view was worth more than the ransom.

There was an old fellow of Gosham,
Who took out his balls to wash 'em,
His wife said "Now Jack,
If you don't put them back,
I'll step on your scrotum and squash 'em."

There was an old abbess quite shocked
To find nuns where the candles were locked.
Said the abbess, "You nuns
Should behave more like guns,
And never go off till you're cocked."

There was an old count of Swoboda
Who would not pay a whore what he owed her.
So, with great savoir-faire,
She stood on a chair
And pissed in his whiskey-and-soda.

There was an old curate of Hestion
Who'd erect at the slightest suggestion.
But so small was his tool
He could scarce fit a spool,
And a cunt was quite out of the question.

There was an old fellow named Art
Who awoke with a horrible start,
For down by his rump
Was a generous lump
Of what should have been just a fart.

There was an old fellow named Skinner
Whose prick, his wife said, had grown thinner.
But still, by and large,
It would always discharge
Once he could just get it in her.

There was an old feminine blighter
Who trained a Chow dog to delight her.
She would cream her own pool
While she sucked off his tool —
How his cock in her cunt would excite her!

There was an old gent from Kentuck
Who boasted a large rubber duck,
But to his dismay,
He had to put it away,
Remembering the night his dick got stuck..

There was an old girl of Kilkenny
Whose usual charge was a penny.
For half of that sum
You could finger her bum—
A source of amusement to many.

There was an old harlot from Dijon
Who in her old age got religion.
"When I'm dead & gone,"
Said she, "I'll take on
The Father, the Son, and the Pigeon."

There was an old hermit named Dave
Who kept a dead whore in his cave.
He said "I'll admit
I'm a bit of a shit,
But look at the money I save."

There was an old lady of Bingly
Who wailed, "I do hate to sleep singly.
I thought I had got
A bloke for my twat,
But he seems rather queenly than kingly."

There was an old lady of Kewry
Whose cunt was a `lusus naturae':
The `introitus vaginae',
Was unnaturally tiny,
And the thought of it filled her with fury.

There was an old lady who lay
With her legs wide apart in the hay,
Then, calling the ploughman,
She said, "Do it now, man!
Don't wait till your hair has turned gray."

There was an old maid from Cape Cod
Who thought all good things came from God.
But it wasn't the almighty
Who lifted her nighty,
It was Roger, the lodger, the Sod.

There was an old man from Bengal
Who liked to do tricks in the hall.
His favorite trick
Was to stand on his dick
While he rolled around on one ball.

There was an old man from Duluth
Whose cock was shot off in his youth.
He fucked with his nose
Or his fingers and toes
And he came thru a hole in his tooth.

There was an old man from South Drum
Whose son was incredibly dumb.
When he urged him ahead,
He got his prick out instead,
For he thought 'ahead' meant suck cum.

There was an old man of Alsace
Who played the trombone with his ass.
He put in a trap
To take out the crap,
But the vapors corroded the brass.

There was an old man of Brienz
The length of whose cock was immense:
With one swerve he could plug
A boy's bottom in Zug,
And a kitchen-maid's cunt in Coblenz.

There was an old man of Cajon
Who never could get a good bone.
With the aid of a gland
It grew simply grand;
Now his wife cannot leave it alone.

There was an old man of Calcutta
Who spied through a chink in the shutter.
But all he could see
Was his wife's bare knee,
And the back of the bloke who was up her.

There was an old man of Connaught
Whose prick was remarkably short.
When he got into bed,
The old woman said,
"This isn't a prick, it's a wart."

There was an old man of Dundee
Who came home as drunk as could be.
He wound up the clock
With the end of his cock,
And buggered his wife with the key.

There was an old man of Duluth
Whose cock was shot off in his youth.
He fucked with his nose
And with fingers and toes,
And he came through a hole in his tooth.

There was an old man of Hong Kong
Who never did anything wrong.
He would lie on his back
With his head in a sack
And secretly fiddle his dong.

There was an old man of St. Bees,
Who was stung in the arm by a wasp.
When asked, "Does it hurt?"
He relied, "No, it doesn't.
I'm so glad that it wasn't a hornet."

There was an old man of Tagore
Whose tool was a yard long or more,
So he wore the damn thing
In a surgical sling
To keep it from wiping the floor.

There was an Old Man of the Mountain
Who frigged himself into a fountain
Fifteen times had he spent,
Still he wasn't content,
He simply got tired of the counting.

There was an old man of the port
Whose prick was remarkably short.
When he got into bed,
The old woman said,
"That isn't a prick; it's a wart!"

There was an old man who said, "Tush!
My balls always hang in the brush,
And I fumble about,
Half in and half out,
With a pecker as limber as mush."

There was an old person of Ware
Who had an affair with a bear.
He explained, "I don't mind,
For it's gentle and kind,
But I wish it had slightly less hair."

There was an old pirate named Bates
Who was learning to rhumba on skates
He fell on his cutlass
Which rendered him nutless
And practically useless on dates.

There was an old satyr named Mack
Whose prick had a left handed tack.
If the ladies he loves
Don't spin when he shoves,
Their cervixes frequently crack.

There was an old Scot named McTavish
Who attempted an anthropoid ravish.
The object of rape
Was the wrong sex of ape,
And the anthropoid ravished McTavish.

There was an old whore from Silesia
Who'd croke: "If my box doesn't please ya,
For a slight extra sum
You can go up my bum
But watch out or my tapeworm'll seize ya."

There was an old whore in the Azores
Whose body was covered with sores.
Why the dogs in the street
Wouldn't eat the green meat
That hung in festoons from her drawers.

There was once a mechanic named Bench
Whose best tool was a sturdy gut-wrench.
With this vibrant device
He could reach, in a trice,
The innermost parts of a wench.

There was once a sad Maitre d'hotel
Who said, "They can all go to hell!
What they do to my wife—
Why it ruins my life;
And the worst is, they all do it well.

There were three ladies of Huxham,
And whenever we meets 'em we fucks 'em,
And when the game grows stale
We sits on a rail,
And pulls out our pricks and they sucks 'em.

Then up spoke a lady from Kew,
And said, as the Bishop withdrew,
"The vicar is quicker
And slicker and thicker,
And longer and stronger than you."

There was an old lady of Gwent,
Whose arse was as big as a tent,
Both cheeks raised protective,
In the middle bisected;
By a pole in the hole somewhat bent!

There's a charming young girl in Tobruk
Who refers to her quiff as a nook.
It's deep and it's wide,
You can curl up inside
With a nice easy chair and a book.

There's a charming young lady named Beaulieu
Who's often been screwed by yours truly,
But now—it's appallin'—
My balls always fall in!
I fear that I've fucked her unduly.

There's a dowager near Sweden Landing
Whose manners are odd and demanding.
It's one of her jests
To suck off her guests —
She hates to keep gentlemen standing.

There's a lovely young lady named Shittlecock
Who loves to play diddle and fiddle-cock,
But her cunt's got a pucker
So it's best not to fuck'er
For when you least expect it, it'll lock.

There's a rather odd couple in Herts
Who are cousins (or so each asserts);
Their sex is in doubt
For they're never without
Their moustaches, and long trailing skirts.

There's a sports-minded coed named Sue,
Who's been coxing the varsity crew.
In the shell Sue is great,
But her boyfriend's irate,
When she calls out the stroke as they screw.

There's a tavern in London that's staffed,
By a barmaid who's tops at her craft:
In her striving to please,
She serves ale on her knees,
So the patrons get head with their draft.

There's a very hot babe at the Aggies
Who's to men what to bulls a red rag is.
The seniors go round
Hanging down to the ground,
And one extra-large Soph has to drag his.

There's a vicar who's classed as nefarious,
Since his shocking perversions are various...
He will bugger some lad
With a dildo (the cad!)
While exulting, "My pleasure's vicarious!"

There's an oversexed lady named Whyte
Who insists on a dozen a night.
A fellow named Cheddar
Had the brashness to wed her-
His chance of survival is slight.

There's an unbroken babe from Toronto,
Exceedingly hard to get onto,
But when you get there,
And have parted the hair,
You can fuck her as much as you want to.

Though his plan, when he gave her a buzz,
Was to do what man normally does,
She declared, "I'm a Soul-
Not a sexual goal!"
So he shrugged and called someone who was.

Though the invalid Saint of Brac
Lay all of his life on his back,
His wife got her share,
And the pilgrims now stare
At the scene, in his shrine, on a plaque.

'Tis a custom in Castellamory
To fuck in the back of a lorry.
The chassis and springs
Are like woodwinds and strings
In the midst of a musical soiree.

To his bride a young bridegroom said, "Pish!
Your cunt is as big as a dish!"
She replied, "Why, you fool,
With your limp little tool
It's like wrapping a nail with a fish!"

To his bride said a numskull named Clarence :
"I trust you will show some forbearance.
My sexual habits
I picked up from rabbits,
And occasionally watching my parents."

To his bride said economist Fife :
"The semen you'll launch as my wife,
We will salvage and freeze
To resemble goat's cheese,
And slice for hors d'oeuvres with a knife."

A couple was fishing near Clombe
When the maid began looking quite glum,
And said, "Bother the fish!
I'd rather coish!"
Which they did — which was why they had come.

As two consular clerks in Madras
Fished, hidden in deep shore-grass,
"What a marvelous pole,"
Said she, "but control
Your bollocks — they're banging my ass."

To his bride, said the sharp eyed detective,
"Can it be that my eyesight's defective?
Is your east tit the least bit
The best of your west tit,
Or is it a trick of perspective?"

Two eager young men from Cawnpore
Once buggared and fucked the same whore.
But her partition split
And the mess and the shit
Rolled out in a pile on the floor.

Under the spreading chestnut tree
The village smith he sat,
Amusing himself
By abusing himself
And catching the load in his hat.

We dedicate this to the cunt,
The kind the broad-minded guys hunt :
All hail to the twat,
Willing, thrilling, and hot,
That wears peckers down, limp and blunt!

When I was a baby, my penis
Was as white as the buttocks of Venus.
But now 'this as red
As her nipples instead—
All because of the feminie genus!

When they asked a pert baggage name Alice,
Who'd been bedded and banged in the palace,
"Was he modest or vain?"
"Was he regal or plain?"
She replied, "He's a jolly good phallus!"

When you fuck little Annie in Anza
You get a great bossom bonanza:
Sucking Annie's soft tits
Makes her throw fifty fits,
And the fuck is a sextravaganza!

While I, with my usual enthusiasm,
Was exploring in Ermintrude's busiasm,
She explained, "They are flat,
But think nothing of that —
You will find that my sweet sister Susiasm."

While out on a date in his Fiat,
The man exclaimed "Where's my key at?"
As he bent down to seek,
She let out a shriek:
"That's not where it's likely to be at."

While spending the winter at Pau
Lady Pamela forgot to say "No."
So the head-porter made her
And the second-cook laid her;
The waiters were all hanging low.

While Titian was mixing rose madder,
His model reclined on a ladder.
Her position to Titian
Suggested coition,
So he leapt up the ladder and had 'er.

Winter is here with his grouch,
The time when you sneeze and you slouch.
You can't take your women
Canoein' or swimmin',
But a lot can be done on a couch.

With his penis in turgid erection,
And aimed at a woman's mid-section,
Man looks most uncouth
In that Moment of Truth,
But she sheaths it with loving affection.

You Women's Lib gals won't agree,
But dependent on men you must be:
You'll need a big 'him',
With a rod firm and trim,
To puggle your water-drains free!

Young Frederick the great was a beaut.
To a guard he cried, "Hey, man, you're cute.
If you'll come to my palace,
I'll finger your phallus,
And then I shall blow on your flute."

You've heard of the bishop of Birmingham,
Well, here's the new story concerning 'im :
He buggers the choir
As they sing "Ave Maria,"
And fucks all the girls whilst confirming 'em

Said the Bishop of Newkey "I've tried,
To get girls to open up wide,
But the sight of my Mitre,
Makes 'em cross their legs tighter,
Thinking what's on my head goes inside!"

When I cogitate said old Mr. Gate,
Tis unfortunate that I have the state,
Of equipment quite small,
A tich of a ball,
And an erection that always comes late.

A widow whose singular vice
Was to keep her late husband on ice
"It's been hard since I lost him —
but I'll never could defrost him!
Cold comfort - , but cheap at the price."

There was a young lady from Hyde
Who ate a green apple and died.
While her lover lamented
The apple fermented
And made cider inside her inside.

There was a young lady from Maine
Who claimed she had men on her brain.
But you knew from the view,
As her abdomen grew,
It was not on her brain that he'd lain.

There was a young lady from Munich
Who had an affair with a eunuch.
At the height of their passion
He dealt her a ration
Of egg white and sundry spewmich

There was a young lady from Norway
Who hung by her heels in a doorway.
She told her young man,
"Get off the divan,
I think I've discovered one more way"

There was a young lady from Prentice
Who had an affair with a dentist.
To make things easier
He used anesthesia,
And diddled her, `non compos mentis'.

There was a young lady from Rheims
Who amazingly pissed in four streams.
A friend poked around
And a fly-button found
Lodged tight in her hole so it seems.

There was a young lady from Rio
Who slept with the Fornier trio.
As she dropped her panties
She said, "No andanties
I want this allegro con brio."

There was a young lady from Spain
Who demurely undressed on a train.
A helpful young porter
Helped more than he orter,
And she promptly cried "Help me again"

There was a young lady from Spain
Who got sick as she rode on a train;
Not once, but again,
And again, and again,
And again, and again, and again.

There was a young lady from Spain
Whose face was exceedingly plain,
But her cunt had a pucker
That made the men fuck her,
Again, and again, and again.

There was a young lady from Troy
Had a moustache, just like a young boy
Though it tickled to kiss
'Twas a source of much bliss
When she used it to brush a man's toy.

There was a young lady from Wheeling
Who claimed to lack sexual feeling.
But a cynic named Boris
Just touched her clitoris
And she had to be scraped off the ceiling.

There was a young lady from Wooster
Who complained that too many men gooster.
So she traded her scanties
For sandpaper panties,
Now they goose her much less than they used 'ter.

There was a young lady in Reno,
Who lost all her dough playing Keno.
But she lay on her back,
And opened her crack,
So now she owns the Casino!

There was a young lady named Alice
Who was known to have peed in a chalice.
'Twas the common belief
It was done for relief,
And not out of protestant malice.

A youthful young curate of Buckingham,
Was chided by girls for not fucking them,
Quoth he "Though my Cock,
Is as hard as a rock,
Your slits are too slack, put a tuck in 'em!"

There was a young lady named Astor
Who never let any get past her.
She finally got plenty
By stopping twenty,
Which certainly ought to last her.

A girl and a boy in a tent,
Were intent on being hell bent,
True, he got an erection,
That she viewed with affection,
But that was as far as they went.

There was a young lady named Blunt
Who had a rectangular cunt.
She learned for diversion
Posterior perversion,
Since no one could fit her in front.

A lady was once heard to weep
"My figure I can no longer keep,
It's my husbands demand,
For a tit in each hand,
And the bastard will walk in his sleep!.

There was a young lady named Bower
Who dwelt in an Ivory Tower.
But a poet from Perth
Laid her flat on the earth,
And proceeded with penis to plough her.

There was a young lady named Brent
With a cunt of enormous extent,
And so deep and so wide,
The acoustics inside
Were so good you could hear when you spent.

There was a young lady named Brook
Who never could learn how to cook.
But on a divan
She could please any man-
She knew every darn trick in the book!

There was a young lady named Cager
Who, as the result of a wager,
Consented to fart
The entire oboe part
Of Mozart's quartet in F major.

There was a young lady named Ciss
Who said, "I think skating's a bliss"
But this she'll never restate,
For a wheel off her skate
Blocked her cunt and now she can't piss

There was a young lady named Clair
Who possessed a magnificent pair;
At least so I thought
Till I saw one get caught
On a thorn, and begin losing air.

There was a young lady named Dot
Whose cunt was so terribly hot
That ten bishops of Rome
And the Pope's private gnome
Failed to quench her Vesuvial twat.

There was a young lady named Duff
With a lovely, luxuriant muff.
In his haste to get in her
One eager beginner
Lost both of his balls in the rough.

There was a young lady named Etta
Who was constantly seen in a swetta.
Three reasons she had:
To keep warm wasn't bad,
But the other two reasons were betta.

There was a young lady named Flo
Whose lover had pulled out too slow.
So they tried it all night,
Till he got it just right...
Well, practice makes pregnant, you know.

There was a young lady named Flynn
Who thought fornication a sin,
But when she was tight
It seemed quite all right,
So everyone filled her with gin.

There was a young lady named Gilda
Who went on a date with a builder.
He said that he would,
And he could and he should,
And he did and it damn well near killed her.

There was a young lady named Gloria,
Whose boyfriend said, "May I explore ya?"
She replied to the chap,
"I'll draw you a map,
Of where others have been to before ya."

There was a young lady named Grace
Who would not take a prick in her "place."
Though she'd kiss it and suck it,
She never would fuck it—
She just couldn't relax face-to-face.

There was a young lady named Hall,
Wore a newspaper dress to a ball.
The dress caught on fire
And burned her entire
Front page, sporting section, and all.

There was a young lady named Hatch
Who would always come through in a scratch.
If a guy wouldn't neck her,
She'd grab up his pecker
And shove the damn thing up her snatch.

There was a young lady named Mable
Who liked to sprawl out on the table,
Then cry to her man,
"Stuff in all you can —
Get your bollocks in, too, if you're able."

There was a young lady named Mandel
Who caused quite a neighborhood scandal
By coming out bare
On the main village square
And frigging herself with a candle.

There was a young lady named Maud,
A terrible society fraud:
In company, I'm told,
She was distant and cold,
But if you got her alone, Oh God!

There was a young lady named May
Who strolled in a park by the way,
And she met a young man
Who fucked her and ran —
Now she goes to the park every day.

There was a young lady named Nance
Who learned about fucking in France,
And when you'd insert it
She'd squeeze till she hurt it,
And shoved it right back in your pants.

There was a young lady named Nelly
Whose tits would jiggle like jelly.
They could tickle her twat
Or be tied in a knot,
And could even swat flies on her belly.

There was a young lady named Ransom
Who was screwed three times in a hansom
When she cried out for more
Said a voice from the floor,
"My name, ma'am, is Simpson, not Samson

There was a young lady named Riddle
Who had an untouchable middle.
She had many friends
Because of her ends,
Since it isn't the middle you diddle.

There was a young lady named Rose
Who fainted whenever she chose;
She did so one day,
While playing croquet,
But was quickly revived with a hose.

There was a young lady named Rose
With erogenous zones in her toes.
She remained animistic
Till a foot-fetishistic
Young man became one of her beaux.

There was a young lady named Schneider
Who often kept trysts with a spider.
She found a strange bliss,
In the hiss of her piss,
As it strained through the cobwebs inside her.

There was a young lady named Smith
Whose virtue was largely a myth.
She said, "Try as I can
I can't find a man
Who it's fun to be virtuous with."

There was a young lady named Twists
Who said she thought fucking a bliss,
For it tickled her bum
And caused her to come
And made her shout louder than THIS!

There was a young lady named Wiled
Who kept herself quite undefiled
By thinking of Jesus;
Contagious diseases;
And the bother of having a child.

There was a young lady of Arden,
The tool of whose swain wouldn't harden.
Said she with a frown,
"I've been sadly let down
By the tool of a fool in a garden."

There was a young lady of Bisector
Who was nicer by far than her sister:
The sister would giggle
And wiggle and jiggle,
But this one would come if you kissed her.

There was a young lady of Brabant
Who slept with an impotent savant.
She admitted, "We shouldn't,
But it turned out he couldn't-
So you can't say we have when we haven't."

There was a young lady of Bode
Who walked down the street in the nude.
A bobby said, "Whetted
Magnificent bottom!"
And slapped it as hard as he could.

There was a young lady of Carmi
Whose housekeeping ways would alarm yaw.
At every cold snap
She would climb in your lab,
So her little base burner could warm yaw.

There was a young lady of Dee
Who went down to the river to pee.
A man in a punt
Put his hand on her cunt,
And God! how I wish it were me.

There was a young lady of Dee
Whose hymen was split into three.
And when she was diddled
The middle string fiddled :
"Nearer My God To Thee."

There was a young lady of Dexter
Whose husband exceedingly vexed her,
For whenever they'd start
He'd unfailingly fart
With a blast that damn nearly unsexed her.

There was a young lady of Dover
Whose passion was such that it drove her
To cry, when you came,
"Oh dear! What a shame!
Well, now we shall have to start over."

There was a young lady of Eagling
And her lover before her was kneeling.
Said she, "Dearest Jim,
Take your hands off my quip;
I much prefer fucking to feeling."

There was a young lady of fashion
Who had oodles and oodles of passion.
To her lover she said,
As they climbed into bed,
"Here's one thing the bastards can't ration!"

There was a young lady of Faze
Who was known to the public as "Jazzed."
Jezebel was her name,
Sucking cocks was the game
She excelled at (so everyone says).

There was a young lady of Gaza
Who shaved her cunt bare with a razor.
The crabs, in a lump,
Made tracks to her rump—
This passing parade did amaze her.

There was a young lady of Gloucester,
Whose friends thought they really had lost her,
Till they found on the grass,
The marks of her arse,
And the knees of the man who had crossed her.

There was a young lady of Kent,
Who admitted she knew what it meant
When men asked her to dine,
And plied her with wine,
She knew, oh she knew — but she went!

There was a young lady of Lincoln
Who said that her cunt was a pickup,
So she had a prick lent her
Which turned it magenta,
This artful old lady of Lincoln.

There was a young man of Kildare,
Who was having a girl in a chair,
At the sixty-ninth stroke,
All the furniture broke,
And his cock went off in mid-air.

There was a young fellow named Locke
Who was born with a two-headed cock.
When he'd fondle the thing
It would rise up and sing
An antiphonal chorus by Bach.

But whether these two ever met
Has not been recorded as yet,
Still, it would be diverting
To see him inserting
His hang while it sang a duet.

There was a young lady of Hill
In an omnibus was taken ill,
So she called the conductor,
Who got in and fucked her,
Which did more good than a pill.

There was a young lady of Twickenham
Who thought men had not enough prick in 'em.
On her knees every day
To God she would pray
To lengthen and strengthen and thicken 'em.

There was a young lady of Wheeling
Said to her beau, "I've a feeling
My little brown jug
Has need of a plug" —
And straightaway she started to peeling.

There was a young lady who said,
As her bridegroom got into the bed,
"I'm tired of this stunt,
That they do with one's cunt,
You can get up my bottom instead."

There was a young lady whose cunt
Could accommodate a small boat or punt.
Her mother said, "Annie,
It matches your fanny,
Which never was that of a runt."

There was a young lady whose thighs,
When spread showed a slit of such size,
And so deep and so wide,
You could play cards inside,
Much to her bridegroom's surprise.

There was a young lass from Surat.
The cheeks of her ass were so fat
That they had to be parted
Whenever she farted,
And also whenever she shat.

There was a young laundress named Wrangle
Whose tits tilted up at an angle.
"They may tickle my chin,"
She said with a grin,
"But at least they keep out of the mangle."

There was a young maiden from Osset
Whose quim was nine inches across it.
Said a young man named Tong,
With tool nine inches long,
"I'll put bugger-in if I lose it."

There was a young man from Bellaire
Who was screwing his girl on the stair.
But the banister broke
So he doubled his stroke
And finished her off in mid-air.

There was a young man from Bengal
Who claimed he had only one ball,
But two little bitches
Pulled down this man's breeches
And proved he had nothing at all.

There was a young man from Biloxi
Whose bowels responded to Moxie.
Drinking glass after glass,
He would tune up his ass,
Till he played like the band at the Roxy.

There was a young man from Dallas
Who had an exceptional phallus.
He couldn't find room
In any girl's womb
Without rubbing it first with Vitalis.

There was a young man from Dundee
Who buggered an ape in a tree.
The results were quite horrid:
All ass and no forehead,
Three balls and a purple goatee.

There was a young man from East Wubley
Whose cock was bifurcated doubly.
Each quadruplicate shaft
Had two balls hanging aft,
And the general effect was quite lovely.

There was a young man from Hong Kong
Who had a trifurcated prong:
A small one for sucking,
A large one for fucking,
And a `boney' for beating a gong.

There was a young man from Glengozzle
Who found a remarkable fossil.
He knew by the bend
And the wart on the end,
'Twas the peter of Paul the Apostle.

There was a young man from Jodhpur
Who found he could easily cure
His dread diabetes
By eating a foetus
Served up in a sauce of manure.

There was a young man from Kent
Whose tool was so long that it bent.
To save himself trouble
He put it in double
And instead of coming, he went.

There was a young man from Lynn
Whose cock was the size of a pin.
Said his girl with a laugh
As she felt his staff,
"This won't be much of a sin."

There was a young man from Maine
Whose prick was as strong as a crane;
It was almost as long,
So he strolled with his dong
Extended in sunshine and rain.

There was a young man from Nantucket
Whose cock was so long he could suck it.
But he looked in the glass,
And saw his own ass,
And broke his neck trying to fuck it.

A petulant whore from Nantucket,
Went down to Hell in a bucket
When asked to come out,
She replied with a shout,
"Arse-holes you buggers — and suck it!"

There was a young man from Peru,
Who took a long trip by canoe.
While staring at Venus,
And rubbing his penis,
He wound up with a handful of goo.

There was a young man from Purdue
Who was only just learning to screw,
But he hadn't the knack,
And he got too far back —
In the right church, but in the wrong pew.

There was a young man from Racine
Who invented a fucking machine.
Concave or convex,
It served either sex,
But oh what a bitch to keep clean.

There was a young man from Rangoon,
Whose farts could be heard on the moon,
When least you'd expect them,
They'd burst from his rectum,
With the force of a raging typhoon.

There was a young man from Salinas
Who had an extremely long penis:
Believe it or not,
When he lay on his cot
It reached from Malta to Martinez.

There was a young man from Seattle
Whose testicles tended to rattle.
He said as he fuck-ed
Some stones in a bucket,
"If Stravinsky won't deafen you — that'll."

There was a young man from Siam
Who said, "I go in with a wham,
But I soon lose my starch
Like the mad month of March,
And the lion comes out like a lamb."

There was a young man from St. Paul's
Who read "Harper's Bazaar" and "McCall's"
Till he grew such a passion
For feminine fashion
That he knitted a snood for his balls.

All loyal Britons will applaud,
A Britain backed bawd name of Maud,
For she went to the States,
Where she charged double rates,
Thus earning many dollars abroad.

There was a young man from 'stamboul
Who boasted so torrid a tool
That each female crater
Explored by this satyr
Seemed almost unpleasantly cool.

There once was a lady from Leicester,
Who said to the man who undressed her,
"If you want a good grind,
Go in from behind,
As the front is beginning to fester."

There was a young man from Tibet-
And this is the strangest one yet-
Whose tool was so long,
So pointed and strong,
He could bugger six Greeks "en brochette".

There was a young man in Havana,
Banged his girl on a player-piana.
At the height of their fever
Her ass hit the lever
And: yes, he has no banana.

There was a young man in Norway,
Tried to jerk himself off in a sleigh,
But the air was so frigid
It froze his cock rigid,
And all he could come was frappe.

There was a young man in the choir
Whose penis rose higher and higher,
Till it reached such a height
It was quite out of sight —
But of course you know I'm just a liar.

There was a young man, name of Saul,
Who was able to bounce either ball,
He could stretch them and snap them,
And juggle and clap them,
Which earned him the plaudits of all.

There's a charming young lady from Newley,
Who's often been fucked by yours truly,
But now — it's appallin',
My balls almost fall in,
I fear I have screwed her unduly!

There was a young soldier from Munich
Whose penis hung down past his tunic,
And their chops girls would lick
When they thought of his prick,
But alas! he was only a eunuch.

There was a young squaw of Wohunt
Who possessed a collapsible cunt.
It had many odd uses,
Produced no papooses,
And fitted both giant and runt.

There was a young man named Crockett
Whose balls got caught in a socket.
His wife was a bitch
So she threw the switch,
And Crockett went off like a rocket.

There was a young man named Hughes
Who swore off all kinds of booze.
He said, "When I'm muddled
My senses get fuddled,
And I pass up too many screws."

There was a young man named Knute
Who had warts all over his root.
He put acid on these
And now when he pees,
He fingers the thing like a flute.

There was a young man named Laplace
Whose balls were made out of spun glass.
When they banged together
They played "Stormy Weather"
And lightning shot out of his ass.

There were three young ladies of Birmingham,
And this is the scandal concerning 'em.
They lifted the frock
And tickled the cock
Of the Bishop engaged in confirming 'em.

Now, the Bishop was nobody's fool,
He'd been to a good public school,
So he took down their britches
And buggered those bitches
With his ten-inch Episcopal tool.

There was a young man named McNamiter
With a tool of prodigious diameter.
But it wasn't the size
Gave the girls a surprise,
But his rhythm — iambic pentameter.

There was a young man named Rex
Who really was small for his sex.
When tried for exposure
The judge's disclosure
Was "de minimus non curat lex."
(the law does not concern itself with small things)

There was a young fellow of Natal
And Sue was the name of his gal,
All the way over,
From Durban to Dover,
He was passing through Suez Canal.

A certain young fella I'm not namin,
Asked a flapper he thought he was tamin,
"Has your maiden still got it's head."
"Don't be foolish." was what she said,
"But I still have the box it came in."

The Archbishop His Grace Lord Bligh,
Had the wife of the Vicar of Casbrigh,
She said "It is rude
To be lewd in the nude."
So he put on his old school tie.

A crusty old Monk of Lahore,
Had a dick a yard long or more,
So he wore the damn thing,
In a surgical sling,
To keep it from wiping the floor.

There was a young man named Zerubbabel
Who had one real, and one rubber ball.
When they asked if his pleasure
Was only half measure,
He replied, "That is highly improbable."

There was a young man named Zerubbabub
Who belonged to the Suck, Fuck & Bugger Club
But the pride of his life
Were the tits of his wife —
One real, and one India-rubber bub.

A brawny young athlete named Grimmon,
Developed a new way of swimmin,
By a marvelous trick,
He could skull with his dick,
Which attracted loud cheers from the women.

There was a young man of Arras
Who stretched himself out on the grass,
And with no little trouble,
He bent himself double,
And stuck his prick well up his ass.

There was a young man of Australia
Who went on a wild bacchanalia.
He buggered a frog,
Two mice and a dog,
And a bishop in fullest regalia.

There was a young man of Belgrade
Who remarked, "I'm a queer piece of trade.
I will suck, without charge,
Any cock, if it's large.
If it's small, I expect to be paid."

There was a young man of Belgrade
Who slept with a girl in the trade.
She said to him, "Jack,
Try the hole in the back;
The front one is badly decayed."

There was a young man of Bombay
Who buggered his dad once a day.
He said, "I like, rather,
Fucking my father —
He's clean, and there's nothing to pay."

There was a young man of Calcutta,
Who tried to write "cunt" on a shutter.
When he got to c-u,
A pious Hindu
Knocked him ass-over-head in the gutter.

There was a young man of Cape Horn
Who wished he had never been born,
And he wouldn't have been
If his father had seen
That the end of the rubber was torn.

There was a young man of Coblenz
Whose bollocks were simply immense:
It took forty-four draymen,
A priest and three laymen
To carry them thither and thence.

There was a young man of Darjeeling
Whose cock reached up to the ceiling.
In the electric light socket,
He'd put it and rock it—
Oh God! What a wonderful feeling!

There was a young man of Devizes
Whose balls were of different sizes.
His tool when at ease,
Hung down to his knees,
Oh, what must it be when it rises!

There was a young man of Dumfries
Who said to his girl, "If you please,
It would give me great bliss
If, while playing with this,
You would pay some attention to these!"

There was a young man of high station
Who was found by a pious relation
Making love in a ditch
To — I won't say a bitch —
But a woman of no reputation.

There was a young man of Khartoum,
The strength of whose balls was his doom.
So strong was his shootin',
The third law of Newton
Propelled the poor chap to the Moon.

There was a young man of Khartoum
Who lured a poor girl to her doom.
He not only fucked her,
But buggered and sucked her—
And left her to pay for the room.

There was a young man of Kutki
Who could blink himself off with one eye.
For a while though, he pined,
When his organ declined
To function, because of a stye.

There was a young man of Lake Placid
Whose prick was lethargic and flaccid.
When he wanted to sport
He would have to resort
To injections of sulphuric acid.

There was a young man of Missouri
Who fucked with a terrible fury.
Till hauled into court
For his bestial sport,
And condemned by a poorly-hung jury.

There was a young man of Natal
Who was fucking a Hottentot gal.
Said she, "You're a sluggard!"
Said he, "You be buggered!
I like to fuck slow and I shall."

There was a young man of Ostend
Who let a girl play with his end.
She took hold of Rover,
And felt it all over,
And it did what she didn't intend.

There was a young man of Ostend
Whose wife caught him fucking her friend.
"It's no use, my duck,
Interrupting our fuck,
For I'm damned if I draw till I spend."

There was a young man of Saskatchewan,
Whose penis was truly gargantuan.
It was good for large whores,
And for small dinosaurs,
And was rough enough to scratch a match upon.

There was a young man of Seattle
Who bested a bull in a battle.
With fire and gumption
He assumed the bull's function,
And deflowered a whole herd of cattle.

There was a young man of St. John's
Who wanted to bugger the swans.
But the loyal hall porter
Said, "Pray take my daughter!
Those birds are reserved for the dons."

There was a young man of Tibet
— And this is the strangest one yet —
His prick was so long,
And so pointed and strong,
He could bugger six sheep en brochette.

There was a young man of Toulouse
Who had a deficient prepuce,
But the foreskin he lacked
He made up in his sac;
The result was, his balls were too loose.

There was a young man with a fiddle
Who asked of his girl, "Do you diddle?"
She replied, "Yes, I do,
But prefer to with two —
It's twice as much fun in the middle."

There was a young man with a prick
Which into his wife he would stick
Every morning and night
If it stood up all right —
Not a very remarkable trick.

His wife had a nice little cunt:
It was hairy, and soft, and in front,
And with this she would fuck him,
Though sometimes she'd suck him —
A charming, if commonplace, stunt.

There was a young man with one foot
Who had a very long root.
If he used this peg
As an extra leg
Is a question exceedingly moot.

There was a young fellow named Skinner
Who took a young lady to dinner
At a quarter to nine,
They sat down to dine,
At twenty to ten it was in her.
(The dinner that is, not Skinner — Skinner was in her
before dinner).

There was a young fellow named Tupper
Who took a young lady to supper.
At a quarter to nine,
They sat down to dine,
And at twenty to ten it was up her.
(Not the supper — not Tupper — It was some son-of-a
bitch named Skinner!)

There was a young fellow of Burma
Whose betrothed had good reason to murmur.
But now that he's married he's
Been using cantharides
And the root of their love is much firmer.

There was a young fellow of Greenwich
Whose balls were all covered with spinach.
He had such a tool
It was wound on a spool,
And he reeled it out inich by inich.

There was a young lady from Drew
Who ended her verse at line two.

But this tale has an unhappy finich,
For due to the sand in the spinach
His bollocks grew rough
And wrecked his wife's muff,
And scratched up her thatch in the scrimmage.

There was a young fellow of Kent
Whose prick was exceedingly bent,
To save him the trouble
He stuffed it in double,
And instead of coming he went.

There was a young fellow of Mayence
Who fucked his own arse in defiance
Not only of custom
And morals, dad-bust him,
But of most of the known laws of science.

There was a young fellow of Perth
Whose balls were the finest on earth.
They grew to such size
That one won a prize,
And goodness knows what they were worth.

There was a young fellow of Strensall
Whose prick was as sharp as a pencil.
On the night of his wedding
It went through the bedding,
And shattered the chamber utensil.

There was a young fellow whose dong
Was prodigiously massive and long.
On each side of his whang
Two testes did hang
That attracted a curious throng.

There was a young German named Ringer
Who was screwing an opera singer.
Said he with a grin,
"Well, I've sure got it in!"
Said she, "You mean that ain't your finger?"

There was a young girl from Annista
Who dated a lecherous mister.
He fondled her titty,
Got one finger shitty,
Then screwed up his courage and kissed 'er.

Ann effete young man of Belgravia,
Cared neither for God nor his Saviour,
He walked down the Strand,
With his Balls in his Hand,
And was arrested for indecent behavior!

There was a young girl from Dundee,
From her fanny there grew a plum tree.
No one ate the nice fruit,
To tell you the truth,
Because they knew it came from her tooty-toot-toot.

There was a young girl from East Lynn
Whose mother (to save her from sin)
Had filled up her crack
With hard-setting shellac,
But the boys picked it out with a pin.

There was a young girl from Hong Kong
Who said, "You are utterly wrong
To say my vagina
Is the largest in China
Just because of your mean little dong."

There was a young girl from Hong Kong
Whose cervical cap was a gong.
She said with a yell,
As a shot rang her bell,
"I'll give you a ding for a dong!"

There was a young girl from Medina
Who could completely control her vagina.
She could twist it around
Like the cunts that are found
In Japan, Manchukuo and China.

There was a young girl from New York
Who plugged up her cunt with a cork.
A woodpecker or two
Made the grade it is true,
But it totally baffled the stork.

Till along came a man who presented
A tool that was strangely indented.
With a dizzying twirl
He punctured that girl,
And thus was the cork-screw invented.

There was a young girl from Peru,
Who noticed her lovers were few;
So she walked out her door
With a fig leaf, no more,
And now she's in bed - with the flu.

There was a young girl from Samoa
Who pledged that no man would know her.
One young fellow tried,
But she wriggled aside,
And he spilled all his spermatozoa.

There was a young girl from Seattle,
Whose hobby was sucking off cattle.
But a bull from the South
Shot a wad in her mouth
That made both her ovaries rattle.

There was a young girl from Siam
Who said to her boyfriend Priam,
"To seduce me, of course,
You'll have to use force,
And thank goodness you're stronger than I am.

There was a young girl from St. Cyr
Whose reflex reactions were queer.
Her escort said, "Mable,
Get up off the table;
That money's to pay for the beer."

There was a young girl from St. Paul
Who went to a newspaper ball.
Her dress caught on fire
And burnt her entire
Front page and sport section and all.

There was a young girl from the coast
Who, just when she needed it most,
Lost her Tampax and bled
All over the bed,
On the head and the beard of her host.

A psychoneurotic fanatic,
Made love to girls in his attic,
He'd whistle a tune,
Bout the cow and the moon,
"When the cow jumps I come — it's dramatic!"

There was a young girl in Berlin
Who eked out a living through sin.
She didn't mind fucking,
But much preferred sucking,
And she'd wipe off the pricks on her chin.

There was a young girl in Berlin
Who was fucked by an elderly Finn.
Though he diddled his best,
And fucked her with zest,
She kept asking, "Hey, Pop, is it in?"

There was a young girl from Dakota
Had a letter from the Pres; he wrote her:
"In addition to gas
We are rationing ass,
And you've greatly exceeded your quota."

A fantastic young prince of Sirocco,
Had erotical penchant rococo,
The cock of this prince,
Was flavoured with quince,
And he seasoned his semen with cocoa.

There was a young girl name McKnight
Who got drunk with her boy-friend one night.
She came to in bed,
With a split maidenhead—
That's the last time she ever was tight.

There was a young girl named Heather
Whose twitcher was made out of leather.
She made a queer noise,
Which attracted the boys,
By flapping the edges together.

I sat next to the Duchess for tea,
It was just as I feared it might be,
Her rumblings abdominal,
Were simply phenomenal,
And everyone thought it was me!

There was a young girl named McCall
Whose cunt was exceedingly small,
But the size of her anus
Was something quite heinous —
It could hold seven pricks and one ball.

There was a young girl named O'Clare
Whose body was covered with hair.
It was really quite fun
To probe with one's gun,
For her quimmy might be anywhere.

There was a young girl named O'Malley
Who wanted to dance in the ballet.
She got roars of applause
When she kicked off her drawers,
But her hair and her bush didn't tally.

There was a young girl named Sapphire
Who succumbed to her lovers desire.
She said, "It's a sin,
But now that it's in,
Could you shove it a few inches higher?"

There was a young girl of Aberystwyth
Who screwed every man that she kissed with.
She tickled the balls
Of the men in the halls,
And pulled on the prongs that they pissed with.

There was a young girl of Angina
Who stretched catgut across her vagina.
From the love-making frock
(With the proper sized cock)
Came Toccata and Fugue in D minor.

There was a young girl of Astoria's
With a penchant for practices curious.
She loved to bat rocks
With her gentlemen's cocks —
A practice both rude and injurious.

There was a young girl of Batonger
who diddled herself with a conger,
When asked how it feels
To be pleasured by eels
She said, "Just like a man, only longer.

There was a young girl of Cah'lina,
Had a very capricious vagina:
To the shock of the fucker
"Twould suddenly pucker,
And whistle the chorus of "Dinah."

There was a young girl of Cape Cod
Who dreamt she'd been buggered by God.
But it wasn't Jehovah
That turned the girl over,
'Twas Roger the lodger, the dirty old codger,
the bugger, the bastard, the sod!

There was a young girl of Cape Town
Who usually fucked with a clown.
He taught her the trick
Of sucking his prick,
And when it went up — she went down.

There was a young girl of Coxsaxie
Whose skirt was more mini than maxi.
She was fucked at the show
In the twenty-third row,
And once more going home in the taxi.

There was a young girl of Darjeeling
Who could dance with such exquisite feeling
There was never a sound
For miles around
Save of fly-buttons hitting the ceiling.

There was a young girl of Des Moines
Whose cunt could be fitted with coins,
Till a guy from Hoboken
Went and dropped in a token,
And now she rattles horribly round the loins.

There was a young girl of Gibraltar
Who was had as she knelt at the altar.
It really seems odd
That a virtuous God
Should answer her prayers and assault her.

There was a young girl of LLewellyn
Whose breasts were as big as a melon.
They were big it is true,
But her cunt was big too,
Like a view of the Straits of Magellan.

There was a young girl of Moline
Whose fucking was sweet and obscene.
She would work on a prick
With every known trick,
And finish by winking it clean.

There was a young girl of Newcastle
Whose charms were declared universal.
While one man in front
Wired into her cunt,
Another was engaged at her arsehole.

There was a young girl of Pawtucket
Whose box was as big as a bucket.
Her boy-friend said, "Toots,
I'll have to wear boots,
For I see I must muck it, not fuck it."

There was a young girl of Pitlochry
Who was had by a man in a rockery.
She said, "Oh! You've come
All over my bum;
This isn't a fuck — it's a mockery."

There was a young idler named Blood,
Made a fortune performing at stud,
With a fifteen-inch peter,
A double-beat metre,
And a load like the Biblical Flood.

There was a young harlot named Schwartz
Whose cock-pit was studded with warts,
And they tickled so nice
She drew a high price
From the studs at the summer resorts.

Her pimp, a young fellow named Biddle,
Was seldom hard up for a diddle,
For according to rumor
His tool had a tumor
And a fine row of warts down the middle.

A silly young man from Peru,
Dreamt he was having it off with a Jew,
He woke up at NIGHT
With a hell of a FRIGHT,
And found it was perfectly true!

There was a young lad from Nahant
Who was made like the Sensitive Plant.
When asked, "Do you fuck?"
He replied, "No such luck.
I would if I could but I can't."

There was a young lad named McFee
Who was stung in the balls by a bee
He made oodles of money
By oozing pure honey
Every time he attempted to pee.

There was a young lady from Bangor
Who slept while the ship lay at anchor
She woke in dismay
When she heard the mate say:
"Let's lift up the topsheet and spanker!"

There was a young lady from Bristol
Who went to the Palace called Crystal.
Said she, "It's all glass,
And as round as my ass,"
And she farted as loud as a pistol.

There was a young lady from Brussels
Who was proud of her vaginal muscles.
She could easily plex them
And so interflex them
As to whistle love songs through her bustles.

There was a young lady from Dumfries
Who said to her boyfriend, "It's some freeze!
My navel's all bare,
So stick it in there,
Before both my legs and my bum freeze."

-oOo—

other POWERFRESH titles

POWERFRESH TONI GOFFE TITLES

1902929411	FINISHED AT 50	2.99 ☐
1902929403	FARTING	2.99 ☐
190292942X	LIFE AFTER BABY	2.99 ☐

POWERFRESH MAD SERIES

1874125783	MAD TO BE FATHER	2.99 ☐
1874125694	MAD TO BE A MOTHER	2.99 ☐
1874125686	MAD ON FOOTBALL	2.99 ☐
187412552X	MAD TO GET MARRIED	2.99 ☐
1874125546	MAD TO HAVE A BABY	2.99 ☐
1874125619	MAD TO HAVE A PONY	2.99 ☐
1874125627	MAD TO HAVE A CAT	2.99 ☐
1874125643	MAD TO BE 40 HIM	2.99 ☐
1874125651	MAD TO BE 40 HER	2.99 ☐
187412566X	MAD TO BE 50 HIM	2.99 ☐

POWERFRESH FUNNYSIDE SERIES

1874125260	FUNNY SIDE OF 30	2.99 ☐
1874125104	FUNNY SIDE OF 40 HIM	2.99 ☐
1874125112	FUNNY SIDE OF 40 HER	2.99 ☐
190292911X	FUNNY SIDE OF 50 HIM	2.99 ☐
1874125139	FUNNY SIDE OF 50 HER	2.99 ☐
1874125252	FUNNY SIDE OF 60	2.99 ☐
1874125279	FUNNY SIDE OF SEX	2.99 ☐

POWERFRESH OTHER A5

1874125171	"CRINKLED "N" WRINKLED"	2.99 ☐
1874125376	A MOTHER NO FUN	2.99 ☐
1874125449	WE'RE GETTING MARRIED	2.99 ☐
1874125481	CAT CRAZY	2.99 ☐
190292908X	EVERYTHING MEN KNOW ABOUT SEX	2.99 ☐
1902929071	EVERYTHING MEN KNOW ABOUT WMN	2.99 ☐
1902929004	KISSING COURSE	2.99 ☐
1874125996	CONGRATULATIONS YOU'VE PASSED	2.99 ☐
1902929276	TOILET VISITORS BOOK	2.99 ☐
1902929160	BIG FAT SLEEPY CAT	2.99 ☐

POWERFRESH SILVEY JEX TITLES

1902929055	FART ATTACK	2.99 ☐
1874125961	LOVE & PASSION 4 THE ELDERLY	2.99 ☐
187412597X	A BABY BOOK	2.99 ☐
1874125996	SHEEP 'N' NASTY	2.99 ☐
1874125988	SPORT FOR THE ELDERLY	2.99 ☐
1902929144	FUN & FROLICS FOR THE ELDERLY	2.99 ☐
1902929756	IT'S A FUNNY OLD WORLD	3.99 ☐
1904967108	WRINKLIES RULE OK!	3.99 ☐

POWERFRESH HUMOUR

1874125945	GUIDE TO SEX & SEDUCTION	3.99 ☐
1874125848	DICK'S NAUGHTY BOOK	3.99 ☐
190292925X	MODERN BABES LB OF SPELLS	4.99 ☐
1902929268	A MUMS LB OF SPELLS	4.99 ☐
1904967000	NOT THE OXFORD DICTIONARY	4.99 ☐
1904967019	PESSIMISIMO	4.99 ☐

1904967027	POLITICAL BOLLOCKS	4
190496706X	POLITICALLY INCORRECT NOTICEBRD	3
1904967124	JIM CRAIG ON GOLF	3
1904967132	JIM CRAIG ON COFFEE	3

POWERFRESH LITTLE SQUARE TITLES

1902929330	LS DIRTY JOKES	2
1902929314	LS DRINKING JOKES	2
1902929322	LS GOLF JOKES	2
190292939X	LS IRISH JOKES	2
1902929292	LS TURNING 18	2
1902929977	LS TURNING 21	2
1902929969	LS THE BIG 30	2
1902929241	LS THE BIG 40	2
1902929233	LS THE BIG 50	2
1902929284	LS THE BIG 60	2
190292973X	LS DO YOU COME HERE OFTEN	2
1902929217	LS YES BUT...!	2
1902929306	LS WHISKY	2
1902929500	LS HOW TO PULL BY MAGIC	2
1904967051	LS PUB GAMES	2
1902929748	LS SEX SLANG	2

POWERFRESH STATIONARY TITLES

1902929381	WEDDING GUEST BOOK	9
1904967094	WEDDING PLANNER	9
1902929349	WEEKLY PLANNER CATS	6
1902929357	WEEKLY PLANNER DOGS	6
1902929365	WEEKLY PLANNER COTTAGES	6
1902929373	WEEKLY PLANNER OFFICE	6
1902929519	HUMDINGER TELEPHONE BOOK	4
1902929527	HUMDINGER ADDRESS BOOK	4
1902929535	HUMDINGER NOTEBOOK	2
1902929810	MODERN BABES ADDRESS BOOK	4
1902929802	MODERN BABES TELEPHONE BOOK	4
1902929829	MODERN BABES BIRTHDAY BOOK	4
1904967043	GARDENERS YEAR BOOK	

Name

Address

P&P £1.00 Per Parcel
Please send cheques payable to Powerfresh LTD
To Powerfresh LTD Unit 3 Everdon Park,
Heartlands Industrial Estate, Daventry NN11 8"